Emerging Champions

By
Elias Cohen

A Draft2Digital Publication

Washington, D.C. – 2025

Emerging Champions

Copyright © 2025 Elias Cohen

All rights reserved. No part of this book may be reproduced, stored in a retrieval system, or transmitted in any form or by any means—electronic, mechanical, photocopying, recording, or otherwise—without prior written permission of the publisher, except in the case of brief quotations used in reviews, articles, or critical essays.

Published by Draft2Digital

Cover design by Joey Johnston

This is a work of nonfiction. The stories and profiles are based on real individuals. Any resemblance to events or people beyond those intentionally profiled is coincidental.

United States of America

Introduction

Introduction

I launched 60'6", a baseball talk show between grandfather and grandson, in April 2023. It turns out–as my ever-humbling sister pointed out–people weren't lining up to listen. Thanks to Emilia's guidance, I pivoted to interviewing up and coming athletes. I started with her freshman year college roommate's little brother, a 13 year old, nationally ranked catcher from Florida. She then put me in contact with then-Vandy Boys freshman star shortstop Camden Kozeal. Come December, the vision had evolved and so did the name. Emerging Champions was born: a series dedicated to sharing the stories of the greatest athletes of tomorrow. Since then, I have interviewed 20 athletes, hosted three live events, and traveled across state-lines for post-game interviews.

This series is not about social media followers or recruiting stars. I wanted to understand how greatness actually begins.

The profiles in this selection are not polished fairytales. Some start on the bench. Others start in frustration, self-doubt, or being overlooked. Each one is a real-time look at growth–messy, personal, and unfinished.

In a sports culture obsessed with instant greatness, I hope these stories remind you that success is a process and sometimes the most meaningful part of an

Emerging Champions
athlete's journey begins before the spotlight ever finds them.

This is about meeting the ones learning how to win–not just once, but for a lifetime.

Let's meet them.
–Elias Benjamin Castillo Cohen

Jordan Smith Jr.

Jordan Smith Jr., Fearlessness

"Erect no artificial walls that might limit potential, stifle creativity, or shackle innovation." -Mike Krzyzewski (Coach K).

Few players embody Coach K's belief more than Jordan Smith Jr., and one moment in the 2024 Virginia State Basketball Championship proves this fact. Late in the 4th quarter with a narrow five point lead, Chance Mallory of St. Anne's Belfield (STAB) turned a fast break into the highlight of his career. The 5'9" University of Virginia committed guard made sure Paul VI's Jordan Smith Jr. ("Smitty") was tight to his hip, which allowed him to gain separation when he did a snatch-back crossover. Jordan stumbled over Mallory's feet and landed on his butt. He quickly got up but not before Mallory jumped through two defenders and spun the ball off the top right of the backboard for a beautiful layup. With one minute and 58 seconds left in the game, Mallory set up the same exact play. He attracted Jordan to his left hip, this time blowing through the paint and aiming to finish with his right hand. Jordan pickpocketed Mallory on his quest to the rim, retrieved the ball, and then pushed through STAB's half court. The play resulted in a fast break foul to give PVI an easy path to closing out the championship game. Jordan refused to be beaten a second time.

Emerging Champions

In today's social media age, it appeared Mallory had the last laugh as world-known brands like Ballislife, Overtime, and Headtap posted his highlight. In fact, this sequence garnered the attention of several Division I programs. Mallory was an overnight sensation. As I scrolled through the comment section to see which NBA stars might have commented something worth mentioning, I instead spotted a laughing emoji adjacent to Jordan's Instagram handle. To Jordan, Mallory's highlight was just another possession. What was different about this play than any other defensive play all year? Jordan put forward the same amount of energy, effort, and focus to this play as he had to all other possessions. I think this play and its repercussions show exactly who Jordan is as a player, one who tries extremely hard on every single possession. I can't tell if he does not take a break, or if he does not need a break. I was reading about Willie Mays in Joe Posnanski's *Baseball 100* and a famous Buck O'Neil quote appeared, *"There were men faster than Willie Mays... But I never saw one faster with a fly ball in the air."* I took my turn to apply this quote to basketball terminology, and unsurprisingly, it matched Jordan's persona perfectly: "There were men faster than Jordan Smith Jr.,... But I never saw one faster with a loose ball on the court."

Not to mention earlier in the Virginia State Championship game, Jordan spun around Mallory, then ferociously two-hand slammed it over STAB's center. This highlight was not posted on Overtime or

Jordan Smith Jr.

Ballislife. I had to watch the full game on Youtube to retrieve this clip. Similar to his consistent play on the defensive end, this highlight dunk became regular. According to my extremely accurate guestimations, he averaged 4.3 incredible fast break dunks with another 2.1 lobs-finished per game.

Why did I include this quote, and more importantly the story for Jordan? They juxtapose each other, right? There are many more stories which display his kindness on and off the court, or his calm energy that allows not one negative thought to enter his mind once tip-off occurs. I could have chosen a story about his leadership, whether on PVI, Team Takeover, or even within his family. Or, his down-to-earthness, which not only referees greatly admire, but also agents or other networkers will appreciate further down the line in his career. From a non-business perspective, his kindness leads him to being known and liked all across the country. After games when his teammates take pictures or sign autographs with fans, Smitty can be seen chatting with his sisters. Not because he thinks he is above the attention–he will never turn down an interview or a picture–but because he would rather spend his time with the family.

For instance, after a game at National Hoopsfest in which PVI shocked the world by beating the consensus number one team IMG Academy, thanks to the sheer will and drive of Jordan, his mom urged him to pack his bags and make his way to the car at the exact

Emerging Champions

moment I requested for an interview. The conversation went something like this[1]:

Elias: "Great game, Jordan. That was the best basketball game I have ever seen. Straight out of a movie. You single handedly beat the best in the nation!"

Jordan: "Hahaha, thanks man. I appreciate it."

Jordan's Mom: "Come on, Jordan. Let's get out of here."

Jordan: "But Mom, this my guy right here. I'm gonna do a quick interview."

Jordan's Mom: (sighing) *"Everyone's* your guy Jordan." (Looks at her watch and as every dedicated mother, makes the sacrifice to wait an extra few minutes for her son).

End Scene!

Thanks for sparingly skimming through my playwriting scene.

---

[1] My playwriting skills are limited but let's see what I can come up with.

Jordan Smith Jr.

Let's get back to the story. [2]I chose a moment about embarrassment, recognition, and energy and started with Coach K's quote because, like always, Coach K was right. In any sport or in life, erecting walls based on inevitable failure or physical weaknesses is to live in fear. Living in fear limits "potential," stifles "creativity," and shackles "innovation." Jordan plays as if he has never once experienced fear, like he skipped that nightmare stage as a child. Jordan never lets his height (~6'3") stop him from guarding a seven-footer. He never lets his bulk inhibit him from guarding an agile guard. There are countless examples of athletes, regardless of their sport, with all the talent in the world, but lack of confidence as a result of playing and living in fear. This lack of confidence diminishes their potential success and future within the sport. Yet again, there are individuals who utilize fear as a driving force within themselves (Most notably being George Brett, the MLB's greatest third basemen of all time), but those athletes do not maximize their potential as human beings. The average 18 year old prospective collegiate or professional basketball player spends 15 hours a week training. I cannot imagine the hours spent in season if you add up commuting times, practices, games, individual training sessions, lifts, homework, and just being a normal teenager. In simple

---

[2] I have texted, emailed, DM'd over 250 prominent and emerging sports figures to schedule an interview. 25-30 would be a solid estimate of how many have responded. 12-15 have actually followed up in scheduling an interview. Jordan has the record for quickest response. He is the only athlete to make a business conversation feel relaxed and informal.

Emerging Champions

terms, for someone to pursue their sport at the highest level, they need to have a strong moral base; one that is not centered around fear. The best players make mistakes. The best players stumble and fall over. The best players do not receive proper recognition. The best players redeem their mistakes, and their highlights always outweigh their lowlights. Jordan is the best.

There is next to no value in my predicting Jordan's athletic future, but I am confident in saying that the floor of his stardom is Jrue Holiday or Victor Oladipo-esque player, a defensive menace and capable scorer which any competing NBA team would love to have on their roster. His ceiling is Jordan Smith Jr.. Call me crazy, but he has the tools and moral base to become a Hall of Fame player, but it is in his hands to personalize his playing-style and reach this apex.

PS: If you need further convincing that he will make it big, here is another funny Jordan story. The basketball community is extremely tight-knit. Everybody knows everybody, especially within the greater DC area. Because of that, I began to ask a question to all of my DC hoopers: "Can you make me your DMV[3] All-Star team, including yourself?" Jalen Rougier-Roane (George Washington) included Jordan in his squad along with Acaden Lewis (Villanova), Derek Dixon (University of North Carolina), and Christian Gurdak (Virginia Tech). Jalen placed Jordan

---

[3] Stands for DC, Maryland and Virginia. Not to be confused with the Department for Motor Vehicles.

Jordan Smith Jr.

at the power forward due to the overload of guards in our region. Rougier-Roane commented, "Shoot, I'm gonna put Smitty at the four because he can do…anything." Jordan is 6'3"[4] and the average height for a power forward in college basketball is 6'8"-6'10". But hey, he is Smitty and Smitty can and will do anything there is to do on a basketball court.

---

[4] After completing an in-person interview, I'd say he is closer to 6'1".

Emerging Champions

Sam Rosand

Sam Rosand, For the Love of the Game

"I ain't ever had a job, I just always played baseball."
–Leroy "Satchel" Paige

After profiling players chasing the spotlight, I turned to someone whose journey has taken an unexpected detour. Sam Rosand, from Landon school in Bethesda, Maryland, is a pitcher whose real strength emerged the moment he could not pitch.

Sam Rosand, without question, was my favorite person to interview. It was my favorite interview because I know how great he is from firsthand experience. Well, of course, I know Jordan Smith Jr. is great. I've seen him dunk on seven-footers before, and he is ESPN number two player in the world for god's sake…but I have never attempted to guard him. This is not to sound cocky because I know I would end up with twisted ankles and on the floor. Arkansas' Camden Kozeal also is great. He hit two home runs during his homecoming game against arguably one of the best pitchers in college baseball, Vandy and now the Brewer's JD Thompson…but I have never attempted to throw a maximum effort 83 mile per hour fastball by him. But Sam Rosand…I know he is great because I faced him for three at-bats, on a freezing, windy, March evening.

Emerging Champions

Early in the 2024 spring season as a first year varsity player for the Maret Frogs, I was ecstatic to face a player of such caliber. Every player in our region wanted a chance to face this guy. I was not being scouted, and frankly did not really care about being made a fool of as long as I got the experience of facing exceptional players. Earlier in the season, Sam pitched a fantastic game against IMG Academy, a top-ten team at the time. He topped 94 mph and unveiled his new slider. [5]Despite anticipating high speeds in my first at-bat, I struggled getting the bat off my shoulders and struck out, something I then-prided myself on rarely doing. I adjusted my mindset for the second at-bat and hoped to attack early, and find that fastball. I fouled off a high and inside fastball. I then fouled-off another fastball. Becoming complacent is a characteristic that is devastating in any sport, but especially in baseball, which is arguably the most mental of them all. With a devilish smirk on my face, I practically dared him to give me another fastball "Come on Sam, you can't blow it by me." This time, he threw a slider that was faster than most fastballs I had seen all season. At least that was the excuse I gave my teammates when I returned to the dugout. I took a cut at it, only to find it in the catcher's glove, an inch off the ground and in the lefty's batters box. I smiled as I took the walk of shame back to the dugout. Our team soon argued as the righties (myself included) complained that the slider was the most viscous pitch

---

[5] Some of yall watch Youth Prospects and will see 14 year old's throwing that hard. That's not even regular for professionals… In 2025, the average MLB fastball was 94.3 mph.

Sam Rosand

we had ever seen and that the lefties were lucky to not see it. The lefties rebutted and claimed his changeup falls off the shelf; time and gravity stop working when he throws it. Both groups refused to believe the other. When I got the chance to sit down and talk to Sam for an hour, I told him about our debate. He confirmed the lefties' statement that changeup is his favorite pitch. I expected a 20 minute account about pitch design or countless hours at the R&D facility in Manassas, Virginia. Instead, I discovered that Sam is not a perfectionist nor a pitch design and velocity freak. He is just a baseball romantic who was blessed with a few convenient growth-spurts and enjoys playing around with new grips.

One of my favorite Sam quotes captures this idea wholly. He first discovered his love for baseball not by playing but by watching. Being a New York fan through and through can be tragic. Just think of the hell they experienced in 2024-2025 alone. The Yankees lost the World Series because of the disastrous 5th inning, including Aaron Judge's dropped catch. Likewise, Jalen Brunson and one of the most complete teams in the NBA fell short to the Indiana Pacers' in buzzer beating fashion. And, let's not forget to mention that the football in New York could not be worse. I could go on for days about how horrible it must be to love sports in New York. Anywho, Sam told me that in the summer of 2019, he attended six straight Jacob DeGrom starts. He said, "At that point, I wasn't really dedicated on playing baseball and going far with it. I was just like, man, I love Jacob Degrom and want to be just like him…"

At first I was nervous about interviewing Sam. I feared he would be reluctant to answer questions since his mind would be circling on the pitcher's nightmare he had just begun living: Tommy John (TJ) Surgery on his ulnar collateral ligament (UCL). TJ surgery attempts to repair the UCL by taking a tendon from your forearm or hamstring to reconstruct the torn ligament. Some pitchers never return and are condemned to obscurity. However, for a select few, they return even better. The most notable success is Justin Verlander. During the 2020 Covid season, Verlander underwent his TJ surgery. Up to that point he was on track to enter baseball's promised land, the Cooperstown Baseball Hall of Fame. The baseball community predicted he would need at least two or three more solid years to reach this pinnacle. Us baseball nerds were heartbroken that one of the best pitchers in the modern day era would almost certainly miss out on his chance at Cooperstown. Not only did he return, but he returned as a better pitcher than he had ever been in the entirety of his career. It is one of the riskiest bets one can make in baseball. A bet that Sam is willing to take and believes he can accomplish. Frankly, one that I believe Sam can accomplish.

Scouts frequently overlook Sam. Perfect Game does not do him justice in their grades and rankings. For that reason, many projected Sam to be drafted no

Sam Rosand

earlier than the third or fourth round. During our interview, he discussed how his surgery made his decision for him and that he is thankful it did. He missed his senior season and was ruled out of the 2025 MLB draft. What impressed me the most was how mature he was about the situation. Although devastating to miss out on opportunities to play in front of MLB scouts and possibly get drafted, Sam viewed surgery as a new opportunity. An opportunity to improve his draft stock and become an even better student of the game. When discussing his plan for returning, Sam mentioned, "My coaches told me to watch guys that replicate my arsenal." He studied how guys like Reece Olsen, Detroit Tiger's up and coming ace, utilized their plus-plus changeup and used the time off to improve the mental side of his game. In fact, I genuinely believe that his surgery was a blessing disguised as a curse. His physical tools are already perfect. What more can you ask for than a 6'2," 200+ pound pitcher, already throwing in the 90s with two wipeout pitches. Having the time to focus only on mentality, coordination, and sequencing will prove how much of a star this kid can become. His path to the MLB will be different, but in the long-run, it should benefit him greatly. I have no doubt that he will immediately impact the University of Missouri's pitching rotation, whether starting or in relief. I expect to watch him fool Volunteer or Commodore batters in the SEC Tournament and the Omaha College World Series in 2026. It is a large bet to place on yourself, but

Emerging Champions

if anyone is capable of succeeding in post-surgery life, it is Sam Rosand.

Sebastion Wilson

Sebastian "Sushi" Wilson, Ambition

"All my life I wanted to be able to do one thing better than anybody else and was very successful. Then I had my accident, and I thought, you know, maybe I can be the best quadriplegic on a respirator that ever lived. And wouldn't you know it, Christopher Reeve goes out and breaks his neck and I'm in competition with Superman."
–Roy Campanella

In recent history, baseball recruitment has evolved, whether you like it or not. No, you can't just Bill-Feller-it and build a baseball stadium in your backyard for MLB scouts to watch your son pitch. You do not just show up and get noticed anywhere. You travel–to regional tryouts, to East Cobb, Georgia for Perfect Game Tournaments, to Jupiter Beach, Florida for showcase exposure, and, if you're elite, to MLB's Combine in Arizona. It is a coast to coast grind from ages 13 through 18. No wonder the Wilson family wants to invest in a private jet. Jokes aside, Sebastian "Sushi" Wilson understands the price–and privilege–of that journey better than most. He has the German graveness and pride of Alexander Zverev, but the Puerto Rican playfulness and sheer joy for the game of Francisco Lindor. Sebastian understands the pressure and urgency to become a star. Reminiscent of a Roy Campanella-esque player, Sushi knows that the world is watching him and expects the utmost excellence, but it never disrupts his eagerness to play the game he loves. This sentiment led him to become the first player in the class of 2027 to commit to a college. Not just any college. Sushi committed to the 2024 Men's College World Series Champion University of Tennessee.

Imagine being a 12 year old baseball fan in 2021. It is a hot July day and with summer ball recently ending, your days, hours, and minutes are left empty. But today is different. Today is the All-Star Game, an American tradition as old as time. It is baseball's July 4th. After contemplating going outside to shoot hoops, you decide to turn on the TV and relax in the air-conditioning. You didn't forget about the All-Star Game, but were tired of seeing the same name that ambushes your Instagram feed by enamored MLB.com writers: Shohei Ohtani. You can't find a way to convince yourself that he is the real deal. You tell your friends he is overrated and that people only like him because he is a decent pitcher and a decent hitter but not great at either. You continue dissing him, but you can't find a way to turn the TV off. Something is just so amazing about Ohtani. You admire that sweeping slider that generated so many whiffs but know that pitchers are supposed to do that. They're supposed to get at least around 70% of the hitters out. Depending on where you lived at this point in time, you would compare him to THE pitcher of your area. For me, it was Max Scherzer. "Max has better movement," I would yell at the TV, right before Shohei would throw a devastating splitter that replicated cartoons, with the

Sebastion Wilson

ball seemingly losing gravity around 5 feet prior to home plate. Everything you said or wished, he would do the exact opposite. Then you saw that smile as he walked off the mound after a scoreless inning. You realize how wrong you were. How could you not like this guy? At this moment, America's youth baseball players decided (if they were hitters) to try pitching, or vice-versa. I felt possessed to mess around with new slider grips and watch Trevor Bauer's tutorials. Shohei inspired a whole new generation of two-way players. Now this is where we get to the tale of Sebastion "Sushi" Wilson.

It is incredible how he never let his pride get intertwined with arrogance. He approached his freshman season of high school baseball with the confidence and maturity of a college commit but with the respect and open-mindedness of a student. Throughout the season, he learned what he could do to help his team win. High School baseball proved to be full of change. Lineup changes were constant, which, in turn, shifted team dynamics. For many players, the cliché of being young, naive, and good to being bullied for challenging the expectations of an upperclassmen's season is true. But not for Sushi Wilson. He had a deep understanding of the concepts of social and team dynamics and understood the strategy like a manager or coach. His joy and obsession for the game was contagious, which allowed for the upperclassmen to appreciate and love his presence.

Emerging Champions

As a sophomore at IMG Academy, baseball's biggest stage, Sushi slashed .526 with nine home runs in just 78 at-bats. That is not just good, that is nation leading production. While his transfer changed not only his geographic location, which is hard enough on most kids, he also had to adjust to a new coaching staff and roster. Sushi rakes. It is as simple as that. No matter the adversity, his poise and production remain.

Sushi's sweet lefty swing meshes that of Gunnar Henderson and Jose Ramirez. His power and speed remind you of Ronald Acuña Jr.. His perfected mechanics and arsenal replicate Craig Krimbrel. His cannon in the outfield instills a vivid memory of Bryce Harper throwing out Marlin base-runners trying to steal an extra base. Then you get to the killer instinct of Barry Bonds. Sushi does not have the aggression of Barry–he is a big sweetheart–but he always takes advantage of an opportunity, most recently being his transfer to IMG. He takes advantage of all opportunities, whether it is a mistake curveball that catches too much of the zone, locating umpire's common mistake-calls, or NIL opportunities given to younger athletes nowadays. He will do all three simultaneously. He'll partner with BWP Bats, then turn around and punish a curveball the next day. That's Sushi Wilson–brand builder, bat-flipper, and future MLB star.

PS: Go to Youtube and type in "USA Prime vs. Wow Factor | 16u Beast of East Championship". You

Sebastion Wilson

will not regret witnessing this Sushi Wilson masterclass

Emerging Champions

Jordan Albarado

Jordan "PorkChop" Albarado, Old School

"Our lives are not determined by what happens to us, but how we react to what happens, not to what life brings us, but by the attitude we bring to life, a positive attitude causes a chain reaction of positive events."
–Wade Boggs

You've got your little league uniform on with nerves bubbling before a big-game. Maybe you've got a rebounding net you haven't quite figured out. Then your dad pulls into the driveway, glove in hand, ready for a quick catch. Suddenly, the tension melts away.

Names carry a weight in sports–just ask jersey manufacturers. Beyond branding, a name can hint at the dreams a father holds for a son. A memorable name leads to higher jersey sales, but a boring one commends you to obscurity. It all starts with a name–a choice parents make, sometimes with ambition in mind. Here are some examples of fathers who knew their children would become stars and named them accordingly: Chipper and Larry Jones, Mickey and Mutt Mantle, Barry and Bobby Bonds, Lonzo/Lamelo and Lavar Ball, and finally Bill and Bob Feller. These fathers not only knew that their kids would become stars, but they made sure of it. Giving Bob and local boys a place to play and be scouted, Bill built Bob a baseball field in their Van Meter, Iowa backyard. Mutt insisted Mickey become a switch hitter, forcing him to practice to the point where Mickey would be scared to come home (maybe not the best parenting). Lavar created a brand for his kids, along with sponsoring Lamelo's semi-professional career in Australia prior to being drafted. The final and most important step in sports parenting is implementing "old-head" views into a small part of your child's game, which sets him above and apart from his teammates. Lavar instilled ball-movement and passing into his boys' game, a basketball strategy which seems to have disappeared since Steve Nash retired. For Mickey Mantle, it was stealing bases, an art form nearing extinction as the power hitter gained popularity in the late 50's. As for Jordan Albarado, it is batting average.

In modern day baseball, batting average is more or less forgotten. Yes, it is a cool and simple stat. Just divide the amount of hits you have by the amount of at-bats and boom, there is your rate of getting a hit or batting average. Throughout baseball history, the community has gone back and forth on the importance of numbers and statistics. Currently, the community understands that batting averages shouldn't be important because Hitter A could go 0-5 with three lineouts to deep left-center and two ground balls down the line where the third baseman magically turns into Brooks Robinson and makes a gold glove play. Hitter B could go 5-5 with 3 bloopers and 2 infield singles. In 2025, obviously the more skilled player is Hitter A. Today, we judge a player based on his average exit velocity or average launch angle. We take the result out

Jordan Albarado

of the picture and focus on mechanical adjustments to see how hard one can hit that five ounce white dot.

However, as many of you have seen or read, Moneyball existed in the early 2000s. Teams hired new scouts, general managers, etc., in order to piece together a group of nine statistically sound guys. In this past era, the perfect lineup was filled by using a few simple stats. The first being OBP, or on-base percentage. This player was your leadoff hitter, generating walks, singles, or pretty much anything to get on base. Behind him, you considered Slugging Percentage, a.k.a the double or home run machine. Batting average was still utilized, but much less than it was in the 20th century. That leads us to the very beginning of statistics: the Ty Cobb and Nap Lajoie batting race. Think of America in 1910. The first things that came to my mind were the three B's: Betting, Baseball, and Beers. Sure enough that was the talk of the 1910 baseball season. At the height of materialism, the new Chalmers vehicle was released, and the CEO, Chalmers himself, declared a free car to the winner of the 1910 batting title. Everyone knew that Ty Cobb, the up and coming line drive hitter, was bound to win it. They placed their bets and gambled their houses on him winning. The Cleveland Spider's Nap Lajoie, the original, more loveable version of Cobb, was a longshot. Especially after coming off a not so great age 34 season. Cobb, unsurprisingly, was in the lead going into the last two games of the season. He sat those two games out, almost certain he would

Emerging Champions

receive that new Chalmers vehicle. Lajoie skeptically, racked up 8 hits in a double header against the St. Louis Browns. Those eight hits put him in the lead for the car. St. Louis manager, Jack O'Conner, most likely had a large sum of money on Lajoie winning that car and put matters into his own hands by allowing him to reach safely eight times. The MLB launched an investigation on O'Conner, and found the perfect way to keep the race "clean", and Lajoie's reputation even cleaner was to give Cobb two extra hits. Cobb won the title. Some suspected treason, but no one could know for certain as newspapers made mistakes and different cities around the country scored differently. For example, in Cleveland, they gave Lajoie a hit on what would have been an error in Detroit. Chalmer decided to give both players a car, and that was that.

While batting average may not be the most important stat nowadays, it has a rich history, one that Jordan "PorkChop" Albarado carries forward into his game. Similar to almost every player in modern baseball society, he hits for exit velocity and launch angle. He has already reached triple digits from his natural right side and is getting extremely close from the left. However, he differs from his peers in batting average. He and his dad have spent countless hours in the batting cage behind their Uvalde home working on outside pitches. In fact, the outside pitch has become his favorite. He believes that it is the easiest pitch to hit as you have more time to hit it than on any other pitch. The ball is practically begging you to slap it the other

Jordan Albarado

way. Jordan will gladly take an 82 mph gap-shot opposed to a 95 mph lineout. You can't score any runs from the dugout.

My best professional comparison is a story I heard about Wade Boggs. After complaining for *years* about being stuck in the minors despite consistently leading the league in average, the Red Sox told him that hitting for average would not get him to the Majors. They reluctantly called him up after his 5th straight year in the Minors. They did not have much choice, as they felt he would demand a trade or retire if he spent one more year without the big-league club. Regardless of his dominance in the Majors, people still questioned his so-called "lack of power." Wade Boggs once told fans that power hitting was easy for him–so easy that he once showed up to batting practice and knocked 12 consecutive home runs. But power was not the point; it was consistency. Jordan lives by this principle.

For some guys, waiting for the middle-middle pitch to go deep just doesn't cut it. For a feared hitter like Wade Boggs or Jordan Albarado, you won't see that middle-middle pitch frequently. When they do see it, of course they will punish it, but waiting on that pitch every at-bat takes away from so many base hits. You are almost guaranteed to see a borderline outside fastball every at-bat in the high school/youth stages of baseball. Why not maximize the number of times you can get on base?

Emerging Champions

I do not believe that scouts rank Jordan properly. He obviously has good base-level numbers, being listed at 5'11" and 205 lbs, with obvious power and defense (1.95 pop-time behind the dish). Unfortunately, scouts cannot wrap their minds around two main things with this kid. The first being that his hand-eye coordination is unteachable. Take a second and think about the great hitting talents of all time with fantastic eyes and high averages. Obviously, Ted Williams will come up first in these discussions. The younger generation will say Juan Soto, as he is our generation's Ted. After those two, there are maybe four other legit contenders for that title: Tony Gwynn, Wade Boggs, Barry Bonds, and Pete Rose. I don't think this talent is underappreciated, but it is so rare that scouts aren't trained to look for it. Imagine you work for a biomechanical engineering firm and your CEO tasks you with searching for fire in water. The task is impossible. It just doesn't work like that (Or so I hope...chemistry was always my weakest subject, so that could be a horrible example), which is why scouts stopped looking for something that really doesn't exist. However, it very much does exist with Jordan. In his freshman season for Uvalde High School, he got 26 hits in 21 games, leaving him with a .441 average. He hit 17 RBI's along with getting walked 20 times. Not to mention his OBP was .562. Then, in his sophomore year, he slashed .466 with three home runs and 25 RBIs. But by far my favorite stat of Jordan's is this: in 18 summer-ball games played between USA Prime and Wow Factor, while facing the best competition in the

Jordan Albarado

nation, Jordan had the same amount of home runs as he did strikeouts, TWO. He is such a natural ball-player that he once hit lefty as a joke with his friends, and they marveled at how smooth the swing looked. He then trained his hand eye coordination with his left hand, and in a matter of months, he began swinging lefty in a local tournament. In his first at-bat, he hit the ball off the top of the wall. Jordan then decided to use this new element of his repertoire in a national tournament. It may have seemed risky as the same scouts which have seen him play for many months were about to watch him swing with his non-dominant hand. If he failed, they could have easily written him off as a jokester or lacking seriousness for attempting a trick that represents showmanship. Instead, he hit the ball 340 feet and over the right field fence. The second reason why Perfect Game and scouts consistently underestimate Jordan is because of his amiability. Being amiable in the sports world is another tool which cannot be taught. From a baseball standpoint, he is the guy that everybody loves. There is a reason why USA Prime teammates go to his house after games to eat steak. There is a reason why the Youth Prospects team always talks to him and follows him around during the pregame. He makes an interview feel like a phone call with your friends. From a business perspective, his easy-going nature will allow him to excel. People just want to be around him. He is underappreciated but never misunderstood. He is able to communicate his goals, intentions, and aspirations clearly. When scouts finally realize the rare blend of plate discipline, natural charm, and communication skills Jordan brings, they will realize what I already know: Jordan Albarado will be a Major League ballplayer

Luke Burns

Luke Burns, Resilience

"Fairy tales do not start, nor do they end, in the dark forest. The son of a gun always pops up smack dab in the middle of the story. But it will all work out. Now it may not work out how you think it will or how you hope it does, but believe me it will work out."
–Ted Lasso

In the fairytale that is soccer, the plot is all jumbled, and the timeline is off the rails. 22 year old seniors battle 19 year old freshmen for a starting spot on the college team. Meanwhile, a 18 year old Lamine Yamal records assists to Robert Lewandowski, a man twice his age. Meanwhile, 14 year old Cavan Sullivan joins the Philadelphia Union MLS team. Through this inconceivable, incomprehensible modern-day timeline of soccer, I have come to the conclusion that there are many fairytale stories throughout the span of a soccer player's career. Unfortunately, I cannot establish much ethos here as Luke Burns was my one and only case study, however, he was one excellent case study.

Born into a soccer family in Scottsdale, Arizona, Luke was destined to be a star. From a young age, he would travel with his family to see his older sister Ansley play in tournaments and showcases. As Luke claimed, and I can attest, having an older sister is the best thing a boy can have while growing up–someone to keep you humble while still being your biggest cheerleader. It is because of her why Luke began to fall in love with the beautiful game. His technical game grew in the soil of his backyard. He would challenge her in any form of skill competition. With Ansley as his teacher and competitor, he learned how to Croif, Maradona, and juggle. In our interview, he later stated that "she would always beat me. She is still better than me with her technical skills."

Similar to most sports but in a higher magnitude, technical skills in the pre-teen age range in soccer tend to vanish. As certain players grow at different rates, the advantage almost always goes to the larger, more developed player. It doesn't matter if you can Croif if the 6'2" brick wall of a twelve year old with a pedo-mustache can push you over just with his presence. Middle school soccer is a lawless wasteland where size beats skill, particularly when 6th graders look like they have mortgages. Luke's zeal for the game disappeared during this era. His coaches quickly noticed his fading passion and frustration and rewarded him with limited playing time. For Luke, the dark forest wasn't a thunderstorm—it was quiet. It was watching other kids take the field while he warmed the bench. It was pretending not to care on the car ride home, earbuds in, eyes out the window. It was questioning whether he still loved the game. On the verge of quitting, his parents and sister took him back to the place where he fell in love… the technical realm of his backyard. Luke's family and coaches worked him harder than he could have imagined.

Luke Burns

Once he reclaimed his starting spot, Luke did not look back. He racked up three stars in a wonderful career at Brophy Prep that included multiple Arizona State Championships and individual accolades. He did two international tours in Barcelona, Spain. He brought life to his club team, the Phoenix Rising FC. After assessing his offers, Luke packed his bags and headed east to the University of Virginia. There challenges emerged yet again. The hot and humid east coast was vastly different from the Arizona desert, and required different training. Of course, being a freshman will also inherently limit your minutes, as well as having a nagging broken arm will grant you next to no playing time. The most beneficial tool an athlete can have is learning how to navigate slumps and dark spots. In his middle school struggles, Luke proved to be a master in maximizing limited opportunities. While challenges did arise throughout the first semester at UVA, they proved to be nothing more than a few speed bumps. Luke earned his first minutes against Rider University in late August. Exactly a month and five days after that game, he secured his first start, playing 45 minutes en route to a 1-0 loss against Stanford, the #2 team in the nation. Only four days later, Luke scored his first collegiate goal. His first goal at UVA wasn't a screamer from distance. It was a gritty, reflex volley that came from a chaotic free kick. The world paused for a second when the ball hit the back of the net. Two weeks after notching his first goal, Luke received a cross on a one-touch to score a beautiful game winner

Emerging Champions

versus American University. Overall, his performances merited him 358 total minutes in his first season.

Beyond the stats, he has this internal volume knob that no one else can quiet. He pushes through physical defenders, runs cross-field, orchestrates give-and-go plays, and is in perfect position to tap the ball into the net. Here is when the knob reaches its max. Luke then sprints adjacent to the sideline and around 5 yards ahead of the flag, he breaks into a knee-slide. In his celebratory moment, he "puts [his] fingers to his cheeks and twists with a big smile on [his] face." For that moment, it is all worth it: the grit and pain, the broken arm, the benching, the pushing, and the hustle.

Luke's story might sound like America's favorite soccer coach Ted Lasso's fairytale, but it's not built on magic. The fine-tuned resilience fueled Luke through every setback and propelled him forward, reminding us all that true strength lies not in how you start but in your relentlessness to keep going.

Jalen Roagier-Roane

Jalen Rougier-Roane, Composure

"I've played a couple of hundred games of tic-tac-toe with my little daughter and she hasn't beaten me yet. I've always had to win. I've got to win."
–Bob Gibson

In the wide realm of sports, there are two kinds of athletes. Those who contain a calm, contagious energy on and off their athletic medium (James Wood, Steven Adams) and those who are fueled by hatred, aggression, and fear (George Brett, Michael Jordan). Then, there is what I like to call an X-Factor player: an athlete who has an on/off switch between these two types. A relaxed player that has extreme control over their mind, body and soul, but will immediately flip the switch to a competitive level, which has a ticking-time bomb within their brain that only is disarmed with a victory. A player of such caliber reminds me of Lionel Messi or Willie Mays. This is an athlete that is so willing to grow and always puts themselves in the best position to win. It is nearly impossible to find a player like this, which is why I struck gold by interviewing Jalen Rougier-Roane.

In June of 2024, I had trouble finding athletes. I had promised fans of Emerging Champions Podcast weekly plans and two interviews per month. Life got busy, and I had not held up my end of the bargain. In fear of becoming random, I sought a big name athlete to make an appearance. After two days of DMing any

Emerging Champions

DC basketball player with over 10,000 followers, I had zero responses to show for it. Time was of the essence, as I had to leave not only my house, but my phone and any contact with the outside world, in eight days for the Virginia Department of Education's World Language Academies, which lasted three weeks. I then stumbled upon Jalen. I find it super interesting and funny how school rivalries inherently form biases. One paints pictures within their brain depicting the most villainous forms of their rival and have trouble seeing an alternate version. Okay, I am getting way too sidetracked, and I should let some legitimate philosopher ponder that theory. The point is I go to Maret. Jalen attended Sidwell. Maret does not like Sidwell. Sidwell does not like Maret. Several NBA players battled against each other on the hardwood of 3000 Cathedral Ave. For example, the Celtics's up and coming star, Luka Garza and the Pelicans's Saddiq Bey. This rivalry has history, so my animosity of Sidwell comes from a well-spirited place. Because of such competitiveness, I had opinions as to what Jalen was like as a person. I have seen him torment the Fighting Frogs on the court for the past 3 years and assumed it was in his nature to be a pest. Regardless of my assumptions, I had days to release an episode and reached out as a last resort. Jalen responded within 15 minutes and we scheduled an interview.

For half an hour, we discussed a variety of topics, ranging from music, to Jalen's role on the Canadian National Team. As much as it pains me to say it, he

Jalen Roagier-Roane

was not that bad of a guy. Okay fine, Jalen was one of the most good-natured athletes I have interviewed, and he presented a balance of eager yet thoughtful responses.

Now that you all have the necessary context, sit back, relax, and enjoy learning about the previously mentioned X-factor players: the athlete with the on and off switch, balancing their competitive aggression and calm demeanor.

Since my first reluctant interaction with him, Jalen has been the most featured athlete ever on Emerging Champions. Because of his generosity, I knew he was the guy to reach out to when planning the first annual Emerging Champions 3v3 Charity tournament. With his help, we pieced together four teams, representing their area of the city (Maret, Sidwell, Bethesda-Chevy Chase, and Flint Hill). With one of his players backing out at the last minute, Jalen reached out to close friend, and popular videographer Ian "Mango" Mangra . The man behind the camera tends to be behind the camera for a reason. That being said, Mango impressed me with his handles and form.

In the first game of the round robin, Jalen's placid demeanor was present. He consistently hit his three-pointers and was never afraid of taking his defender to the rim, but you could tell just by watching that there was no ferocity or urgency in his game. In an effort to build his friend's confidence, he dished the

Emerging Champions

ball to Mango multiple times, hoping he would sink one. After a few unsuccessful attempts, Jalen became scrappy. As the Bethesda Chevy Chase boys inched closer to victory, Jalen set up an isolation play. He slowly dribbled the ball up the light-wash wood floor, then burst into an in-n-out, hesitation pull-up jumper. He noticed the trajectory of the ball was too strong, almost begging to be bounced off the back-rim. He ran to his spot, pushed through numerous box-out efforts, and tipped the ball back to himself before passing to a wide-open Caleb Gillus. Caleb sank his three-pointer to win the game for Sidwell.

As good as he was in casual settings, Jalen's truest version–his most explosive, urgent self–was saved for the 2024 DC State Championship. Jalen and the Sidwell team had a chance to make history and win the state title for the third straight year, solidifying themselves as one of DC's greatest dynasties, which holds extreme weight in a city with such a storied basketball history. Some of the greatest players to emerge from the DC area include: Dematha's Victor Oladipo, Jerami Grant, and Markelle Fultz, along with Oak Hill Academy's 34 NBA players, most notably, Kevin Durant and Carmelo Anthony. To be in the likes of these NBA icons as one of the winningest players of the DC area means a great deal. To understand the magnitude of Jalen's heroics in this State Championship game, we must first dive into his history in the previous two championship games.

Jalen Roagier-Roane

In 2022 as a freshman starter, Jalen contributed what NBA scouts like to call "3 and D", which is when a player can shoot the ball well from distance and play a disciplined defense but not much else. These players tend to be role players that good teams like to use off their bench. Incomplete projects, yet still valuable. Jalen's steady defense was key in the low scoring State Championship against Jackson-Reed. However his offensive touch vanished, as he only scored two points. The only memorable part of this game was current Georgetown star Caleb Williams's remarkable buzzer-beating put back layup to win the game. Fast forward to 2023, and the Sidwell Friends team returned to the finals, playing a near-identical Jackson-Reed team. Jalen contributed a respectable 11 points in their larger-margin-of-victory win; however, a knee injury sidelined him later in the game. He limped through the celebration and while he was overjoyed with his team's performance, he seemed unsatisfied with the way his year ended. A year later, on March 3, 2024, at 8 pm, Jalen sat calmly with his headphones on, as he watched his classmates on the Sidwell Women's team lose a nailbiter in the women's final.

The '23-24 season started off on the worst possible foot for this Sidwell men's team. After two consecutive years of brilliance, Sidwell's schedule included tournaments against nationally ranked prep schools and out of conference star-stacked rosters. They lost two of their first four games. Before conference play they battled against Wizard's rookie Tre Johnson at

Emerging Champions

Link Academy and later Bullis, but they could not finish the job. Sure, they won every game after the January 6th loss to Bullis, but the doubts that circled Sidwell's early season blues remained in Jalen's mind before the championship tipped off. As a junior, high expectations surrounded his production, and the team's success could not be reliant on a 3 and D player or one with an injured knee. Coach Singletary, the team, and even the fans would soon find out that Sidwell looked sluggish. Acaden Lewis, the DMV's next NBA star, could not find his shot to begin the game. His beautiful passes made up for his inefficient shooting in the first half. Sidwell's freshman big Ian Condon had trouble keeping up with St Johns's lengthy and more mature frontcourt. Even four year star Caleb Williams could not find his groove until later in the game, shooting five for nine.

They were down 21-20 at halftime. Jalen flipped the switch. It was his turn. In a program as talented as Sidwell's, it can be difficult to know when it is your time to assume responsibility. Jalen did not just assume responsibility, but he took over the game. He began the third quarter by signaling for shooter Jake Williams to throw him a lob. His back-door cut left both St John's forwards clueless. He summoned all of his strength as the penultimate step powered his way upwards. It seemed he would never land. That is, of course, until he caught the ball. With all the aggression built up in his body, he sent the ball flying through the same net which he would later cut the last string off of as the

Jalen Roagier-Roane

Championship MVP. His defensive prowess kicked in and St. John could only manage to score 6 points in the quarter. His fourth quarter three-pointer sealed the deal and left St. Johns with no other choice but to foul and let Sidwell win via the free throw. Jalen is the X-factor that powered Sidwell to their third straight state championship. Luckily, this time he knew it. The emotions poured out of him, as he cried holding the trophy and his teammates bombarded him with love and appreciation.

Although the X-factor switch was always inside of him, this was the first time he showcased it. Since then, Jalen has not let go. That attribute led to his playing for Team Canada in his age group at the FIBA World Cup, as well his commitment to play at Division I George Washington University. Jalen's basketball evolution has been incredible to watch and will only continue to grow exponentially. His composure–honed, earned, and paired with fire–is what makes Jalen unstoppable

Emerging Champions

Closing Reflection

Closing Reflection

I've recorded episodes that I almost didn't publish. I've sent over 200 DMs that went unanswered. I've been ghosted by around 30 athletes who initially said yes and then disappeared. I've had videos that reach hundreds of thousands, and some that barely reach 100. I've worked with, dapped up, interviewed, texted, played against, and joked with countless athletes that are bound for their respective professional leagues. Something was just different about these six. Every one of these stories challenged what I thought an "emerging champion" should look like. None of them fit perfectly in a box. That's why they stayed with me. I did not write these to predict greatness. I wrote them because each athlete made me pause. A trait. A divergence. A turning point. Something that felt bigger than athletic capability.

Smitty taught me that leadership does not come from being the loudest on the team but from listening with a ferocious, fearless kindness.

Sam reminded me of the nostalgia of being a baseball romantic and how a growth mindset turns every setback into leverage.

Sushi taught me to weaponize ambition and challenge every opportunity, every single time.

Porkchop brought back a lost art, one I hold close to me throughout my baseball career.

Emerging Champions

Luke proved that slumps build resilience, which helps far beyond sports.

Jalen showed me how to flip the switch–from quiet to fierce, calm to storm–on command.

If you took anything from these pages, I hope it is this:

The best athletes don't just train to win. They train to evolve.

And evolution is *always* a story worth sharing.

–Elias

Overtime

JORDAN SMITH JR Q&A

WHEN DID YOU CATCH YOUR FIRST IN-GAME DUNK?
IT WAS PROBABLY THE END OF MY 6TH GRADE YEAR. I WAS AROUND 5'11.

HOW WOULD YOUR COACHES AND TEAMMATES DESCRIBE YOU?
A DOG.

HOW DO YOU KEEP COMPOSURE WHILE LEADING YOUR TEAM AGAINST NUMBER ONE IMG?
THIS WASN'T NOTHING NEW TO US. WE'VE BEAT IMG AND OTHER #1S BEFORE AT HOOPSFEST. YOU GOTTA JUST STAY CALM WHEN YOU COME OUT HERE AND DON'T LET THE CROWD GET TO YOU.

YOU ARE THE DMV'S PUTBACK KING. HOW DOES IT FEEL TO MAKE THESE ABSURD PLAYS?
I MEAN ITS ALRIGHT. PUTBACK OR NOT PUTBACK, LAYUP OR NO LAYUP. YOU JUST GOTTA PLAY HARD.

Emerging Champions

SAM ROSAND

HOW DO YOU THROW YOUR CHANGEUP?
I THROW A SPLIT-CHANGE. SO YOU GOTTA HOLD IT LOOSE, KINDA LIKE AN EGG. I'M JUST A NATURAL PRONATOR SO IT WORKS OUT WELL FOR ME.

WHY DID YOU CHANGE YOUR SLIDER?
ANYTIME YOU CAN GET A BREAKING PITCH WITH MORE VELOCITY IT'S GONNA BE HARDER FOR HITTER TO HIT. I REALIZED WHEN I GOT ON THE SIDE OF THE BALL IT WAS SHARPER THAN WH. I'M UNDER IT.

ARE YOU EVER GONNA COME BACK TO BEING TWO-WAY?
OH NO. NO NO NO. FRESHMAN YEAR I HAD TWO HITS IN A SCRIMMAGE, BUT I HAD A SHORT PRIME. WE GOT INTO LEAGUE PLAY, AND I WENT ZERO FOR SOMETHING. I SAID COACH, YOU A GONNA WANNA TAKE ME OUT.

Overtime

SEBASTIAN "SUSHI" WILSON

WHO IS YOUR BIGGEST FAN?
I WOULD SAY MY BROTHER. EVEN THOUGH HE DOESN'T SHOW IT A LOT, I KNOW HE REALLY LOVES ME. HE'S ALWAYS IN THE PACKED CAR COMING TO ALL MY GAMES.
WHEN YOU PITCH DOES IT MAKE YOU A BETTER HITTER?
I CAN SEE THE UMPIRE'S TENDENCIES. I FEEL LIKE KNOWING HOW PITCHERS GET YOU OUT MAKES YOU A BETTER HITTER.
HOW DO YOU DEAL WITH THE SACRIFICE?
I FEEL LIKE THE SACRIFICES HAVE TO BE MADE IF YOU WANNA MAKE THE NEXT JUMP. MY PARENTS HAVE MADE TRAVELING SACRIFICES FOR ME, SO I UNDERSTAND THE REALITY AND DEAL WITH IT.

Emerging Champions

JORDAN "PORKCHOP" ALBARADO

IS THE OUTSIDE PITCH STILL YOUR FAVORITE EVEN WHEN HITTING LEFTY?
OH NO. THAT INSIDE PITCH. WHEN IT COMES TO ME IT JUST LOOKS LIKE A BIG OLE BEACH BALL, AND I SWING AS HARD AS POSSIBLE.

WITH NIL HOW DOES IT FEEL FOR WHEN COMPANIES TO REACH OUT TO YOU?
I'M IN A SMALLER TOWN, SO I'VE NEVER GOTTEN AS MUCH AS THE OTHERS. BUT DOING THE THINGS THAT PEOPLE ARE SEEING IS AWESOME. I WOULD HAVE NEVER THOUGHT I'D BE HERE TWO YEARS AGO BUT I WORK SUPER HARD, SO I'M GLAD IT IS COMING.

DO YOU SEE A BIG DIFFERENCE IN HIGH SCHOOL VS TRAVEL BALL?
I HAVE TO MAKE A LOT OF ADJUSTMENTS IN THE WAY I THINK. THE VELO I SEE IN TEXAS I HAVE A TARGET ON MY BACK. BUT IN SUMMER BALL I GOTTA GET USED TO THE VELO. IN SUMMER BALL I KEEP THE ENERGY GOING WITH ALL OF OUR CELLYS.

Overtime

LUKE BURNS

How did you work up the ladder at UVA?
Over the summer I came up to campus early for captain's practice. I didn't know how freshman year would go, if I would redshirt, play at all. But when I got the chance I kept it.

Other than soccer, which UVA sport do you go and watch?
I love watching the women's soccer team play. When I'm not there, the swimming team is really good here.

Who is your professional comparison?
There's a player in the Prem...Emil Smith Rowe. He works very hard offensively and defensively and I try to replicate everything he does.

Emerging Champions

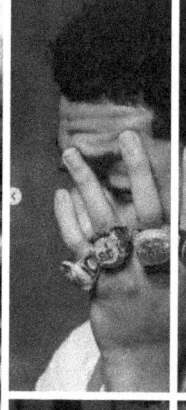

WHAT IS ON YOUR PREGAME PLAYLIST?
RECENTLY I'VE JUST BEEN LISTENING TO FUTURE. THE PAST TWO ALBUMS HAVE BEEN ON REPEAT.

DOES THAT MEAN YOU ARE ON KENDRICK'S SIDE?
I'M NOT ON KENDRICK'S SIDE THOUGH. I FEEL LIKE I'VE GOT TO REP DRAKE BECAUSE OF MY CANADIAN NATIONAL TEAM STUFF. IN THE U18S THEY WOULD ALWAYS PLAY HIS DISS-TRACK WHENEVER WE ENTERED THE BUILDING.

DO YOU HAVE THAT ONE TEAMMATE YOU CANNOT LOOK AT WHEN COACH IS TALKING?
THE FUNNY THING ABOUT THAT IS THAT SOMETIMES THAT TEAMMATE MIGHT BE ME. I CAN BE SERIOUS IN THE MOMENT, BUT IT CAN GET TOO FUNNY.

JALEN ROAGIER-ROANE

Acknowledgements

Acknowledgements

This book would not exist without the athletes who generously shared their time, trust, and stories. Jordan Smith Jr, Sam Rosand, Sebastian Wilson, Jordan Albarado, Luke Burns, and Jalen Roagier-Roane, you are the reason this project mattered. Thank you for letting me explore and discuss what drives you, scares you, and the challenges you face and carry into your daily competition.

To the families, coaches, and teammates that helped shape these athletes–your influence is evident and major. These champions are only the culmination of the environment which you have curated for them.

Thank you to the listeners of the podcast. Your feedback, curiosity, and belief are all the motivation I have needed to continue this important era of my life.

Thank you to the early readers. Your editing help and honest feedback helped me never settle for 'good-enough.'

Thank you to Aunt Melinda and Uncle David for getting me *The Baseball 100* for Christmas two years ago. I hope this project honors the spirit of sports writing that Joe Posnanski's book instilled in me.

Emerging Champions

Bibliography

Bibliography
Jordan Smith Jr.:
Zoom Interview, January 29, 2024
In Person Interviews, February 25, 2024 and December 8, 2024

Sam Rosand:
In Person Interview, July 23, 2024

Sebastian Wilson:
Zoom Interview, January 12, 2024

Jordan Albarado:
Zoom Interview, May 24, 2024

Luke Burns:
Zoom Interview, November 6, 2024

Jalen Roagier-Roane:
Zoom Interview, June 19, 2024
3v3 Charity Tournament, Aug 27, 2024

www.ingramcontent.com/pod-product-compliance
Ingram Content Group UK Ltd.
Pitfield, Milton Keynes, MK11 3LW, UK
UKHW011420211025
8504UKWH00001B/63